HIGHER EDUCATION ACT REAUTHORIZATION: A COMPARISON OF CURRENT LAW AND S. 1642

HIGHER EDUCATION ACT REAUTHORIZATION: A COMPARISON OF CURRENT LAW AND S. 1642

CHARMAINE MERCER,
BLAKE ALAN NAUGHTON,
REBECCA R. SKINNER, DAVID P. SMOLE,
JEFFREY J. KUENZI
AND RICHARD N. APLING

Novinka Books
New York

For permission to use material from this book please contact us:
Telephone 631-231-7269; Fax 631-231-8175
Web Site: http://www.novapublishers.com

NOTICE TO THE READER

The Publisher has taken reasonable care in the preparation of this book, but makes no expressed or implied warranty of any kind and assumes no responsibility for any errors or omissions. No liability is assumed for incidental or consequential damages in connection with or arising out of information contained in this book. The Publisher shall not be liable for any special, consequential, or exemplary damages resulting, in whole or in part, from the readers' use of, or reliance upon, this material.

This publication is designed to provide accurate and authoritative information with regard to the subject matter covered herein. It is sold with the clear understanding that the Publisher is not engaged in rendering legal or any other professional services. If legal or any other expert assistance is required, the services of a competent person should be sought. FROM A DECLARATION OF PARTICIPANTS JOINTLY ADOPTED BY A COMMITTEE OF THE AMERICAN BAR ASSOCIATION AND A COMMITTEE OF PUBLISHERS.

LIBRARY OF CONGRESS CATALOGING-IN-PUBLICATION DATA

Higher Education Act reauthorization : a comparison of current law and S. 1642 / Charmaine Mercer ... [et al.].
        p. cm.
  Includes bibliographical references and index.
  ISBN 978-1-60456-955-1 (softcover : alk. paper)
  1. United States. Higher Education Act of 1965. 2. Universities and colleges--United States--Finance. 3. Federal aid to higher education--United States. 4. Educational law and legislation--United States. 5. Student aid--Government policy--United States. I. Mercer, Charmaine.
  KF4225.H53 2008
  344.73'074--dc22
                            2008032042

Published by Nova Science Publishers, Inc. ✦ *New York*

CONTENTS

PREFACE

The Higher Education Act of 1965 (HEA) as amended, authorizes the federal government's major federal student aid programs (Title IV), as well as other programs which provide institutional aid and support (Titles II, III and V). In addition, the HEA authorizes services and support to less-advantaged students (select Title IV programs), and to students pursuing international education and certain graduate and professional degrees (Titles VI and VII). The programs authorized by the HEA are administered by the U.S. Department of Education (ED), and made available an estimated 70% ($94 billion) of all federal, state and institutional aid awarded to postsecondary students in 2005-2006 (excluding tax benefits)[1].

The HEA was last comprehensively reauthorized by the Higher Education Amendments of 1998 (P.L. 105-244), which expired September 30, 2003. Since the initial expiration of the authorization, there have been several temporary extensions[2]. Most recently, the HEA was extended by the First Higher Education Extension Act of 2007 (P.L. 110-44), which authorizes the programs and activities of the HEA through July 31, 2007.

The 108th and 109th Congresses each considered but did not complete the HEA reauthorization process. For the 110th Congress, the Higher Education Amendments of 2007 (S. 1642) was introduced by Senator Kennedy on June 18, 2007, and approved by the Senate Health, Education, Labor, and Pensions Committee (HELP) on July 10th. Additionally, much like what occurred during the 109th Congress, this year the reauthorization of the HEA has become heavily intertwined with the budget reconciliation process, as both the Senate HELP Committee and the House Education and Labor Committee have reported budget reconciliation bills that would make numerous changes to programs and provisions contained in the HEA.[3]

This report provides a side-by-side comparison of the HEA reauthorization proposal in the HELP Committee-passed version of S. 1642 to current law. The side-by-side is generally organized to correspond with the organization of S. 1642.[4] The report begins with a brief overview of the titles and major programs of the HEA, and includes a short summary of the larger issues and proposed changes in S. 1642 for each title and program.

It is important to note that the side-by-side comparison, which is presented in Table 1, is intended to provide a summary of the larger issues and changes addressed in S. 1642 as they compare to current law. Thus, this analysis does not attempt to capture all of the changes of the proposed bill. Finally, S. 1642 includes provisions that extend the authorization of appropriations for most HEA programs through FY2013. In this report, proposed authorization periods will only be noted for those programs and provisions that have a different authorization period. It should otherwise be assumed that appropriations would be authorized through FY2013. Unless otherwise specified, "such sums as may be necessary" would be authorized for most programs.

This report will be updated following major legislative developments.

OVERVIEW [*]

There are seven titles of the HEA that authorize numerous programs and provisions designed to provide assistance to postsecondary students and institutions. The seven titles of the HEA are

- Title I — General Provisions
- Title II — Teacher Quality Enhancement
- Title III — Institutional Aid
- Title IV — Student Assistance
- Title V — Developing Institutions
- Title VI — International Education Programs; and
- Title VII — Graduate and Postsecondary Improvement Programs

Title I

Title I primarily provides the general provisions and definitions that govern most of the programs authorized by the HEA. For example, it includes many of the institutional reporting requirements, important definitions such as "institution of higher education" (IHE) and "distance education," and authorizes a performance based organization (PBO) to administer federal student aid within ED. The major changes proposed include:

---

[*] This report is excerpted from CRS report #RL34095, July 23, 2007

- Changes to the definitions of an IHE, including eliminating the requirement that proprietary institutions earn at least 10% of their revenue from non-Title IV sources (referred to as the 90/10 rule) as a condition of Title IV eligibility.
- The establishment of new requirements related to making college tuition information available to the public, including the development of higher education price indices and net price calculators.

Title II

Title II is the source of grants for improving teacher education programs, strengthening teacher recruitment efforts and training for prospective teachers. This title also includes the reporting requirements for states and IHEs regarding quality of teacher education programs. The major changes proposed include:

- The elimination of the State and Recruitment grants and all Title II-A funds are directed to the current Partnership grant program.
- The introduction of additional accountability, evaluation, and reporting requirements regarding traditional teacher preparation programs and the introduction of new requirements for programs offering alternative routes to certification.

Titles III and V. Titles III and V are the primary sources of institutional support authorized by the HEA. Both titles award grants to IHEs to strengthen their academic, administrative, and financial capabilities. Title III includes provisions for IHEs that serve large numbers of needy students, tribal colleges and universities, Alaska Native and Native Hawaiian-serving institutions, and historically black colleges and universities. Title V authorizes funds for Hispanic-serving institutions. The major changes proposed include:

- The establishment of a new program, the Native American-serving non-tribal institution program.
- The establishment of the Promoting Postbaccalaureate Opportunities for Hispanic Students program.

Title IV

Programs authorized under Title IV are the primary source of federal aid to support postsecondary education. The largest Title IV student aid programs are the Pell Grant program and the Federal Family Education Loans (FFEL) and the William D. Ford Direct Loan (DL) programs. Additionally, there are several other smaller student aid programs, Federal Supplemental Educational Opportunity Grants (FSEOG), Federal Work-Study (FWS), and Federal Perkins Loans — collectively known as the campus-based programs, and the Leveraging Educational Assistance Partnership (LEAP). Title IV also authorizes programs for student services. The federal TRIO programs and the Gaining Early Awareness and Readiness for Undergraduate Programs (GEAR UP) both provide less-advantaged students with support services to help them complete high school, and enter and persist through college. The major changes proposed include:

Part A: Grants to Students

- The elimination of the tuition sensitivity provision from the Pell Grant program.
- The provision of up to two Pell Grant awards in a single academic year for students who enroll at least half-time in a four-year or two-year institution.
- Broadened eligibility for Academic Competitiveness and National Science and Mathematics Access to Retain Talent (SMART) grants to include students who are enrolled half-time, pursuing a one-year or two-year certificate, or are enrolled in programs that require five years of study.

Part B: Federal Family Education Loan Program

- Additional requirements pertaining to the disclosure of additional information to borrowers regarding the capitalization of interest on federal student loans and the consequences of consolidating federal student loans.
- An increase in the FFEL program lender loan origination fee from 50 to 100 basis points for consolidation loans.

Part E: Perkins Loans

- The expansion of the types of public service occupations for which Perkins Loans may be canceled.

Part F: Need Analysis

- An expansion of the definition of room and board to include a room and board allowance for students who live in housing located on a military base or who receive a basic allowance for housing.
- The exclusion of the value of military housing or a military housing allowance received by a student or his/her parent, from consideration as untaxed income or benefits in the need analysis formula.

Part G: General Provisions

- The addition of several requirements regarding the information IHEs must make available to enrolled and prospective students, including the institution's transfer of credit policy, campus emergency response and evacuation policies, fire safety practices and standards, and information on student body diversity, completion and graduation rates, employment of graduates, and students' pursuit of graduate school.

Part H: Program Integrity

- The addition of several new accreditation provisions including those related to the stated mission of the IHE, distance education, public disclosure of an IHE's transfer of credit policy, and due process requirements for an IHE opposing an adverse action taken by an accrediting agency.

Title VI

Title VI authorizes a variety of grants to IHEs and related entities to enhance instruction in foreign language and area studies. The international education program reflects the special priority placed by the federal government on foreign language and area studies, especially with respect to diplomacy, national security, and trade competitiveness. The major changes proposed include:

- Making undergraduate students engaged in intermediate or advanced study eligible for fellowships currently limited to graduate students.

Title VII

There are three graduate fellowship programs authorized under Title VII targeted to select graduate and professional degrees.

In addition to these seven titles, prior amendments to the HEA have included additional titles which established free-standing programs and provisions, or amended existing authorities outside of the HEA. S. 1642 would add a new title to the HEA, Title VIII — Miscellaneous (authorizing 13 new programs), and Title IX — Amendments to Other Laws would amend existing authorities outside of the HEA. These two titles are preceded by S. 1642 in this report to denote that they are not a part of the HEA.

Table 1. Comparison of Current Law with S. 1642

Current Law	S. 1642 (as reported by the Senate Committee on Health, Education, Pensions, and Labor)
Title I: General Provisions.	
Institutions of Higher Education (IHEs).	
Selected provisions from the Section 101 definition of an IHE:	Includes the following changes to this definition:
• Admits as regular students only individuals who have a certificate of graduation from a secondary school or its recognized equivalent; persons above the age of compulsory attendance may also be admitted as regular students. • An IHE must provide a program for which the institution awards a bachelor's degree or provides not less than a two-year program of study that is acceptable for full credit toward a bachelor's degree.	• Expands criteria for students who may be admitted as regular students to include students dually enrolled in an IHE and a secondary school. • Expands criteria for institutional eligibility under Section 101 to IHEs that provide a degree that is acceptable for admission to a graduate or professional degree program if reviewed and approved by the Secretary.
Graduate medical schools located outside the United States (U.S.) may participate in the Federal Family Educational Loan (FFEL) program if: (1) the institution meets specific requirements related to student enrollment and passing rates on a particular examination; or (2) the institution has a clinical training program that was approved by a state as of January 1, 1992.	Changes the second set of criteria to require that the institution has continuously operated a clinical training program in at least one state that is approved by that state.

Table 1. Continued

Current Law	S. 1642 (as reported by the Senate Committee on Health, Education, Pensions, and Labor)
To participate in Title IV, both proprietary institutions and postsecondary vocational institutions must admit as regular students, only individuals who have a certificate of graduation from a secondary school or its recognized equivalent. Persons above the age of compulsory attendance may also be admitted as regular students.	Expands criteria of students who may be admitted as regular students to include students dually enrolled in an IHE and a secondary school.
Definitions.	
No similar provision.	Defines "critical foreign language" as each of the languages contained in the list of critical languages designated by the Secretary of Education (Secretary) in the August, 2, 1985 *Federal Register*, except that with respect to a specific title of the HEA, the Secretary may set priorities based on the purposes of the title, national security, economic competitiveness, and the educational needs of the U.S.
No similar provision.	Defines "distance education" as education that uses one or more specific types of technologies to deliver instruction to students who are separated from their instructor and to support regular and substantive interaction between students and their instructor.
No similar provision.	States that the term "poverty line" means poverty line as defined in the Community Service Block Grant Act.

Table 1. Continued

Current Law	S. 1642 (as reported by the Senate Committee on Health, Education, Pensions, and Labor)
Protection of Student Speech and Association Rights.	
A sense of Congress addresses the protection of student speech and association rights.	Expands the current sense of Congress in several ways, including specifying that IHEs should design their academic programs in accordance with their education goals; colleges should facilitate the free and open exchange of ideas; students should not be intimidated, harassed, or discouraged from speaking out; and students should be treated "equally and fairly." Modifies existing language to require that the imposition of any sanctions of students be done "objectively and fairly."
National Advisory Committee on Institutional Quality and Integrity (NACIQI).	
The Secretary appoints the 15 members of NACIQI for three-year terms of office. The committee advises the Secretary in several areas related to accreditation, including providing guidance related to the establishment and enforcement of the standards of accrediting agencies for Title IV purposes, advising the Secretary regarding the recognition of a specific accrediting agency, developing and recommending standards and criteria for specific categories of institutions for which no recognized accrediting agency exists, making recommendations related to the eligibility and certification process, and advising the Secretary regarding the relationship between accreditation and eligibility and certification, and IHEs and state licensing.	Renames NACIQI the *Accreditation and Institutional Quality and Integrity Advisory Committee.* Retains the 15 committee member structure, but 5 members would be appointed by the Secretary, 5 members appointed by the House of Representatives, and 5 members appointed by the Senate. Each member serves for six years. Retains all of the functions of the committee authorized by current law, except it eliminates developing standards and criteria for specific categories of institutions for which no recognized accrediting agency exists.

Table 1. Continued

Current Law	S. 1642 (as reported by the Senate Committee on Health, Education, Pensions, and Labor)
Drug and Alcohol Abuse Prevention.	
No similar provision.	Requires IHEs to determine the number of drug and alcohol-related incidents and fatalities that occur on the IHE's property or as part of the IHE's activities and are reported to the IHE. It also requires IHEs to determine the number and type of sanctions imposed in response to drug and alcohol-related incidents and fatalities that occur on the IHE's property or as part of the IHE's activities.
College Tuition Information for Consumers.	
No similar provision.	Requires the Commission of the Bureau of Labor Statistics (BLS) to develop higher education price indices that accurately reflect the annual change in tuition and fees for undergraduate students enrolled in specific types of IHEs (e.g., four-year public degree-granting). Requires the Secretary to annually publish a national list and a list for each state that ranks IHEs based on their changes in tuition and fees over the preceding two years. Data must be reported by institutional sector (i.e., level and control of the institution). Data must also be reported based on the percentage change in tuition and fees and the dollar change in tuition and fees. IHEs whose increase in tuition and fees exceeds that of its applicable higher education price index would be placed on the "Higher Education Price Increase Watch List."

Table 1. Continued

Current Law	S. 1642 (as reported by the Senate Committee on Health, Education, Pensions, and Labor)
No similar provision.	Requires the Secretary to annually report for each state a comparison of the percentage change in state appropriations per enrolled student in public IHEs to the percentage change in tuition and fees for each public IHE for each of the five previous years.
No similar provision.	Requires the Secretary to report on the total amount of need-based aid and merit-based aid provided by the state to students enrolled in each public IHE.
No similar provision.	Requires the Secretary to develop net price calculators for each institutional sector no later than one year after the date of enactment. Not later than three years after the date of enactment, IHEs receiving federal funds under the HEA must adopt and use a net price calculator developed by ED or by the IHE.
No similar provision.	Requires an IHE receiving funds authorized by the HEA to include in its application materials the most recent information regarding the net price of the institution calculated for each income quartile based on the income of the students' parents (dependent students) or the income of the students (independent students) for each of the two academic years preceding the academic year for which the application is produced.

Table 1. Continued

Current Law	S. 1642 (as reported by the Senate Committee on Health, Education, Pensions, and Labor)
No similar provision.	Requires the Secretary to contract with an independent organization with expertise in the development of consumer-friendly websites to recommend improvements to the College Opportunities On-Line (COOL) website. No later than one year after the date of enactment, the Secretary must implement these recommendations.
No similar provision.	Requires the Secretary to create a model document, the University and College Accountability Network (U-CAN), that IHEs may use to annually report basic institutional information. IHEs are not required to participate in this data collection effort.
No similar provision.	Requires the Government Accountability Office (GAO) to examine the institutional cost burden associated with completing the Integrated Postsecondary Education Data System.
Student Information Databases.	
No similar provision.	Prohibits the development of a federal database of student information. This prohibition does not extend to the development of state databases of student information.
Performance Based Organization (PBO).	
Establishes that the Performance-Based Organization (PBO) shall be a discrete management unit responsible for managing the operational functions supporting the programs authorized under Title IV.	Establishes that the functions of the PBO in ED are now referred to as "administrative and oversight" functions, not "operational." The PBO will also be responsible for the administration of federal student financial assistance programs

Table 1. Continued

Current Law	S. 1642 (as reported by the Senate Committee on Health, Education, Pensions, and Labor)
No similar provision.	Directs the PBO to utilize procurement systems that streamline operations, improve internal controls, and enhance management.
Requirements for Lenders and Institutions Participating in Educational Loan Arrangements.	
No similar provision.	Requires lenders that provide FFEL or Direct Loans (DL) and that are also financial institutions as defined in Section 509 of the Gramm-Leach-Bliley Act to provide several disclosures to students, in writing, prior to making a loan to a student, such as interest rate and repayment options. Also requires these lenders to annually report to the Secretary any reasonable expenses paid or given under specific sections of the HEA to any employee in the financial aid office of any Title IV eligible IHE that receives any federal funding or assistance (referred to as "covered institutions"). The Secretary must subsequently report this information to the authorizing committees.

Table 1. Continued

Current Law	S. 1642 (as reported by the Senate Committee on Health, Education, Pensions, and Labor)
No similar provision.	• Requires the Secretary to report on the adequacy of the information provided to students and their families about educational loans.
	• Directs the Secretary to develop a model format for use by lenders and covered institutions to report information about educational loans.
	• Requires lenders to annually provide to the Secretary and to each covered institution with which it has a student loan arrangement, the information included in the model format for each type of loan provided to students (or their parents) attending a covered institution.
	• Requires covered institutions to submit an annual report to the Secretary that includes the information provided to the institution by each lender with which the covered institution has a student loan arrangement and a detailed explanation of why the institution believes the terms and conditions of each loan are beneficial to students.
	• The covered institution must also make this report publicly available and provide the report to students and their families in time for the student or parent to take the information into account in selecting or applying for a student loan.

Table 1. Continued

Current Law	S. 1642 (as reported by the Senate Committee on **Health, Education, Pensions, and Labor**)
Title II: Teacher Quality Enhancement.	
Teacher Quality Enhancement Grants for States and Partnerships.	
Funds appropriated for Title II, Part A are for state, partnership, and recruitment grants.	Eliminates the state and recruitment grants.
Defines a "high-need local educational agency (LEA)" as one that serves a school in, "an area in which there is (A) a high percentage of individuals from families with incomes below the poverty line; (B) a high percentage of secondary school teachers not teaching in the content area in which the teachers were trained to teach; or (C) a high teacher turnover rate."	Amends the definition of a "high-need" LEA as one that (1) enrolls at least 20% or 10,000 children from low-income families; or (2) serves only schools designated with a locale code of 6, 7, or 8 and has a total enrollment of less than 600 children; and (3) has a high percentage of out-of-field or out-of-grade-level teachers; or (4) has a high teacher turnover rate or a high percentage of teachers with emergency, provisional, or temporary certification.

Table 1. Continued

Current Law	S. 1642 (as reported by the Senate Committee on Health, Education, Pensions, and Labor)
Authorizes the Secretary to award competitive grants to eligible partnerships. Requires funds to be used for implementing reforms of teacher preparation programs, providing clinical experience including mentoring of prospective teachers, and providing professional development that improves content knowledge for current teachers. Allows funds to be used for preparing teachers to work with diverse populations, involving parents in program reform, disseminating information, coordinating reform efforts, developing school management and leadership, and recruiting new teachers into the profession.	• Authorizes the Secretary to award competitive grants to eligible partnerships. Requires funds to be used for carrying out a program for the pre- baccalaureate preparation of teachers, a teaching residency program, or both. Proposed program (as revised) is very similar to the current partnership program but adds considerably more detailed language on accountability and use of funds for reforms. • Expands the required uses of funds for clinical experience and adds new required uses for induction, support, and recruitment. • Adds new language describing a teaching residency program that gives new teachers and prospective mid-career professionals a one-year stipend to receive intensive training toward a Master's degree and requires that they teach for a period of at least three years in a high-need school. • The program would also give experienced teachers the opportunity to serve as mentor teachers in exchange for full relief from their usual teaching duties.
Grantees may receive an award under each of the state, partnership, and recruitment programs only once.	Partnerships may receive only one grant during a five-year period; however, an eligible partner may be a member of multiple partnerships.

Table 1. Continued

Current Law	S. 1642 (as reported by the Senate Committee on Health, Education, Pensions, and Labor)
Requires the Secretary to ensure equitable geographic distribution of the grants throughout the U.S..	Requires the Secretary to ensure an "equitable geographic distribution of grants among rural and urban areas."
Requires grantees to provide matching funds, from non-federal sources, in an amount equal to 25% of the grant for the first year of the grant, 35% for the second year, and 50% for each succeeding year.	Requires grantees to provide matching funds, from non-federal sources, in an amount equal to 100% of the amount of the grant and gives the Secretary authority to waive this requirement for any fiscal year in which it would result in serious hardship or an inability to carry out the authorized activities.
Requires that all IHEs that conduct traditional teacher preparation programs and enroll students receiving federal assistance under the HEA report the status of pass rates for teacher preparation students taking assessments within three years of leaving the program, program and accreditation information, designation of low-performing programs, among other things.	Adds programs that offer alternative routes to state certification and licensure to the list of programs that must report this information. Requires programs to report "scaled scores" in addition to pass rates of those still enrolled in a program or who have completed in the last two years, to disaggregate program information by race and gender, and to describe activities employed to prepare teachers to use technology.
States must annually submit a report card on the quality of teacher preparation to the Secretary.	Prohibits the Secretary from creating a national list or ranking states or schools based on these reports.

Title III: Institutional Aid

Strengthening Institutions.

Secretary may award grants to any eligible institution with an application approved under section 351 (Minority Science and Engineering Improvement Program).	Expands eligibility to include any eligible institution with an application approved under all other sections of Title III.

Table 1. Continued

Current Law	S. 1642 (as reported by the Senate Committee on Health, Education, Pensions, and Labor)
	Expands authorized activities to include remedial education, English language instruction courses, and education or counseling services designed to improve financial literacy and economic literacy of students or students' parents, among other things.
American Indian Tribally Controlled Colleges and Universities.	
Tribal College or University (TCU) has the same meaning as tribally controlled college or university in Section 2 of the Tribally Controlled College or University Assistance Act of 1978 (TCCUAA) and includes institutions listed in the Equity in Educational Land-Grant Status Act of 1994 (EELGSA).	Defines a TCU as: an institution that qualifies for funding under the TCCUAA or the Navajo Community College Assistance Act of 1978 or, is cited in section 532 of the EELGSA.
No similar provision.	Expands authorized activities to include acquisition of real property and education or counseling services designed to improve financial literacy and economic literacy of students or students' parents, among other things.
The Secretary shall ensure maximum and equitable distribution of funds among all eligible institutions.	Establishes a new allocation formula whereby the Secretary can reserve 30% of the appropriation for one-year construction grants. Remaining funds should be allocated as follows: 60% based on Indian student count and 40% equally distributed among eligible TCUs. The minimum grant would be $500,000.

Table 1. Continued

Current Law	S. 1642 (as reported by the Senate Committee on Health, Education, Pensions, and Labor)
Alaska Native and Native Hawaiian-Serving Institutions.	
No similar provision.	Expands the authorized activities to include education or counseling services designed to improve financial literacy and economic literacy of students or students' parents, among other things.
Native American-Serving, Non-Tribal Institutions.	
No similar provision.	Establishes a new program (Section 318) for Native American-serving, non-tribal institutions. Native American defined as: an individual who is of a tribe, people or culture indigenous to the U.S.. Eligible institutions must have at least 10% Native American students and cannot be a TCU as defined in Section 316. Minimum grant would be $200,000.
Historically Black Colleges and Universities (HBCUs).	
The phrase "professional and academic areas in which Blacks are underrepresented" shall be determined by the Secretary and the Commissioner of the BLS, on the basis of the most recent available satisfactory data, as professional and academic areas in which the percentage of Black Americans who have been educated, trained, and employed is less than the percentage of Blacks in the general population.	Requires the Secretary to also consult with the Commissioner for Education Statistics.

Table 1. Continued

Current Law	S. 1642 (as reported by the Senate Committee on Health, Education, Pensions, and Labor)
No similar provision.	Expands the authorized activities to include education or counseling services designed to improve financial literacy and economic literacy of students or students' parents, among other things.
Provides formula for allotting funds.	Adds new requirement that to receive the annual allotment, HBCUs must annually provide data on the following: number of Pell Grant recipients, number of graduates from the preceding year, and the number of students who enrolled in a graduate or professional program within last five years.
Historically Black Colleges and Universities, Professional or Graduate Institutions.	
No similar provision.	Expands the authorized activities to include education or counseling services designed to improve financial literacy and economic literacy of students or students' parents, among other things.
There are 18 existing eligible grantees.	Expands the list of eligible graduate and professional schools/programs (Part B, Section 326) to include Alabama State University; Coppin State University; Delaware State University; Prairie View A&M University; Langston University; West Virginia State University; and Fayetteville State University.
Historically Black College and University Capital Financing Program.	
No similar provision.	Requires the Secretary to submit an annual report to the authorizing committees no later than 90 days after the date of enactment, that provides ED's progress in implementing the recommendations made by the GAO for improving the HBCU Capital Financing Program.

Table 1. Continued

Current Law	S. 1642 (as reported by the Senate Committee on Health, Education, Pensions, and Labor)
Title IV: Student Assistance.	
Federal Pell Grants.	
Existing program authority expired in FY2004. The most recent authorized maximum Pell Grant (Pell) award is $5,800 for academic year 2003-2004.	The program authority for Pell is extended to 2013. The authorized maximum Pell award is as follows: $5,400 for academic year 2008-2009; $5,700 for 2009-2010; $6,000 for 2010-2011; and $6,300 for 2011-2012.
If the maximum appropriated Pell award is greater than $2,700, tuition sensitivity is invoked. As implemented by ED, tuition sensitivity reduces the Pell for a small number of low-income students attending IHEs with very low tuition charges.	Eliminates tuition sensitivity provision.
Minimum authorized Pell award is $400.	Changes the minimum Pell award to 10% of the appropriated maximum Pell award, unless a recipient qualifies for an award between 5% and 10% in which case recipient would receive 10%.
No similar provision.	Provides up to two Pell Grant awards in a single academic year for students who enroll at least half-time in a four-year or two-year institution.
No similar provision.	Limits Pell receipt to 18 semesters or equivalent determined by Secretary. Limit is determined without regard for attendance status (full-time or part-time) and would include time prior to the date of enactment.

Table 1. Continued

Current Law	S. 1642 (as reported by the Senate Committee on Health, Education, Pensions, and Labor)
Academic Competitiveness (AC) and Science Mathematics Access to Retain Talent (SMART) Grants.	
Secretary is authorized to award grants to Pell-eligible U.S. citizens, who are enrolled full-time in an undergraduate program. First and second year undergraduates receive an AC grant and students in their third or fourth year receive a SMART grant.	Removes the term "academic" from all references to year of study in the AC and SMART grant program provisions. Extends eligibility to eligible non-citizens and those enrolled on at least a half-time basis.
First-year students who were previously enrolled in an undergraduate program are ineligible for AC or SMART.	Extends eligibility to first-year students who were previously enrolled in a program of undergraduate education.
No similar provision.	Extends eligibility to students enrolled in certificate programs lasting at least one year (AC grant) or lasting at least two years (SMART grant).
No similar provision.	Extends eligibility for SMART grants to students studying qualified subjects who are enrolled in IHEs that do not permit declaration of a major.
No similar provision.	Extends a fifth year of eligibility for SMART grants to students in programs that require five full years of course work.
No similar provision.	Requires that IHEs make payments for AC and SMART grants in the same manner as Pell .

Table 1. Continued

Current Law	S. 1642 (as reported by the Senate Committee on Health, Education, Pensions, and Labor)
Federal TRIO Programs.	
Authorizes the Secretary to award grants for the following TRIO programs: Talent Search, Upward Bound, Student Support Services, McNair Postbaccalaureate Achievement, and Educational Opportunity Centers for a four-year period with a minimum grant amount between $170,000 and $190,000.	Extends the grant period to five years and increases the minimum grant amount to $200,000.
No similar provision.	Requires the Secretary to establish outcome criteria for measuring the quality and effectiveness of the TRIO programs. Outcome criteria must be disaggregated by the following categories: low-income, first generation, and individuals with disabilities. Further requires that programs be assessed on how they meet or exceed their objectives as measured against an eligible entity's stated target outcomes.
Authorizes numerous services for TRIO programs, including assistance with academic matters, applications for college admission, financial aid, and personal and career counseling.	Creates a new set of required services for each of the TRIO programs that includes assistance with academic matters, applications for college admission, financial aid, and financial literacy.
No similar provision.	Establishes priority for Upward Bound projects that include at least 30% of first-time students who have a high risk of academic failure. Prohibits the Secretary from denying participation in Upward Bound to a student who enters the program for the first time after the ninth grade.

Table 1. Continued

Current Law	S. 1642 (as reported by the Senate Committee on Health, Education, Pensions, and Labor)
Secretary is authorized to award contracts to evaluate the effectiveness of the TRIO programs and disseminate the results of these evaluations.	Requires the Secretary to submit an annual report on the program's delivery of services, participating students' secondary and postsecondary school enrollment and completion, and academic performance. The report must include the following: • Disaggregated data by individual project performance, including descriptive, longitudinal, and multi-cohort information, and be comparable to the national population of low-income, first generation students and students with disabilities. • National performance data with the primary purpose of identifying and highlighting best practices for increasing college access and persistence through implementation of the programs. Secretary prohibited from requiring an eligible TRIO grant applicant to recruit students to serve as a control group in an evaluation. However, the Secretary is allowed to give priority to entities that voluntarily elect to participate in an evaluation using a control group.
Gaining Early Awareness and Readiness for Undergraduate Programs (GEAR UP).	
The Secretary is required to give priority to eligible entities that previously carried out GEAR UP programs prior to the Higher Education Amendments of 1998.	Eliminates this priority.

Table 1. Continued

Current Law	S. 1642 (as reported by the Senate Committee on Health, Education, Pensions, and Labor)
Requires the Secretary to allocate at least 33% of available funds for both State and Partnership grants.	Eliminates this requirement and requires the Secretary to consider the geographic distribution and the distribution of awards between urban and rural applicants.
Limits the amount of funds that State and Partnership grantees can use for early intervention to not less than 25% and not more than 50% of the amount available for distribution.	Applies this limitation only to State grantees.
No similar provision.	Grantees must ensure that grants will be used to supplement and not supplant federal, state and other local funds used for similar activities and programming.
Eligible entities must submit a plan to the Secretary which contains a description of "the activities for which assistance is sought" and "provides such additional assurances as the Secretary determines necessary."	Specifies that the contents of an application must include a description of how the entity meets the scholarship requirements, a description of how the entity meets the scholarship requirements, a demonstration of adequate staffing for coordinating activities, an assurance that activities would not displace employees or eliminate positions at schools, a description of how the entity defines the targeted cohort and serves the cohort through grade 12, and a description of program coordination with existing federal, state, and local projects.
Requires State grantees to establish and maintain a scholarship component that provides students with funds equal to 75% of the state's cost of attendance (COA) or the maximum Pell award.	Requires grantees to notify students of the eligibility requirements to receive a scholarship and to create or organize a trust for each cohort of students. Gives the Secretary authority to allow State grantees to exceed the 50% use of funds for early intervention.

Table 1. Continued

Current Law	S. 1642 (as reported by the Senate Committee on Health, Education, Pensions, and Labor)
Federal Supplemental Educational Opportunity Grants (FSEOG).	
The Secretary is authorized to allocate up to an amount equal to 10% of the amount by which funds appropriated for programs authorized under Title IV, Part A exceeds $700 million, among IHEs from which 50% or more Pell recipients either graduate or transfer to four-year IHEs.	Removes this provision.
The allowance for books and supplies used in calculating each institution's average COA for purposes of allocating funds to IHEs according to "fair share" allocation procedures is $450.	Increases the allowance for books and supplies to $600.
Leveraging Educational Assistance Partnership (LEAP) Program.	
Grants to students may not exceed $5,000 per academic year.	Increases maximum grant per academic year to the lesser of $12,500 or the student's COA.

Table 1. Continued

Current Law	S. 1642 (as reported by the Senate Committee on Health, Education, Pensions, and Labor)
The Special Leveraging Educational Assistance Partnership (SLEAP) program is authorized funding from amounts appropriated for HEA, LEAP that are in excess of $30 million. State SLEAP programs may consist of the following activities: increasing the dollar amount of grants under the LEAP program; carrying out transition programs from secondary school to postsecondary education for needy students; carrying out early intervention, mentoring, and career education programs; and awarding merit or academic scholarships to needy students. The federal share of funds may not exceed 33a% and states must meet maintenance of effort requirements.	Replaces the SLEAP program with the "Grants for Access and Persistence" program. The program is authorized in the same manner as SLEAP. • Authorized activities include (a) partnerships with IHEs, private corporations, philanthropic organizations, and other entities to coordinate financial assistance to low-income students; (b) need-based grants to low-income students for access and persistence, (c) early notification of low-income students about their eligibility for financial aid, and (d) encouraging the participation of low-income students in early information and intervention mentoring, or outreach programs. • States must apply in partnership with private corporations or philanthropic organizations, and IHEs. • The federal share of funds is 50% for states that apply in partnership with IHEs whose combined enrollment represents less than half of all students enrolled in the state; and 57% for states that apply in partnership with IHEs whose combined enrollment represents more than half of all students enrolled in the state.

Table 1. Continued

Current Law	S. 1642 (as reported by the Senate Committee on Health, Education, Pensions, and Labor)
Robert C. Byrd Honors Scholarship Program.	
Merit-based scholarships are awarded to high school students who demonstrate academic achievement and show promise of continued achievement.	Expands eligibility to include home-schooled students.
Child Care Access Means Parents in School.	
The Secretary is authorized to provide grants to assist IHEs in providing campus-based child care services to low-income students.	Specifies a minimum grant award of $30,000 when annual appropriations exceed $20 million. Also, expands definition of a low-income students to include those who would be eligible for Pell but for enrollment in graduate level programs or for temporary U.S. status.
Learning Anytime Anywhere Partnerships.	
The Secretary is authorized to make grants to partnerships to enhance the delivery and quality of career-oriented lifelong learning through technology.	Program is repealed.
Federal Family Education Loan (FFEL) Program and William D. Ford Direct Loan (DL) Program.	
No similar provision.	Lenders must provide borrowers of unsubsidized Stafford Loans who are eligible for a deferment with information on how the capitalization of interest may impact the total amount to be repaid.

Table 1. Continued

Current Law	S. 1642 (as reported by the Senate Committee on Health, Education, Pensions, and Labor)
Certain restrictions on inducements, mailings, and advertising apply to guaranty agencies.	Restrictions on inducement, payments, mailings, and advertising by guaranty agencies are revised to include other items, such as stock or other securities, prizes, travel, entertainment expenses, and tuition payment. The prohibition on unsolicited mailings is revised to apply to mailings by postal or electronic means. Guaranty agencies are prohibited from performing or paying another person to perform any function the IHE is required to perform under Title IV, Parts B, D, or G.
Guaranty agreements must contain certain provisions regarding the form of forbearance granted by lenders.	Requires lenders to provide borrowers with specific information when granting forbearance, including information about the impact of the capitalization of interest; and, at least once every 180 days, information on the accrual of interest.
Certain requirements apply to agreements with lenders regarding consolidation loans.	Lenders must, in a clear and conspicuous manner, disclose to borrowers who consolidate loans that were made under Title IV, Parts B, D, or E information on any loan benefits that would be lost by consolidating their loans.
The Secretary, guaranty agencies, lenders, and subsequent loan holders are required to enter into agreements with credit bureaus to exchange information concerning student borrowers.	Replaces "credit bureaus" with "consumer reporting agencies;" and also requires reporting of the type of loan, the repayment status of the loan, and any other information required by federal law.

Table 1. Continued

Current Law	S. 1642 (as reported by the Senate Committee on Health, Education, Pensions, and Labor)
Eligible lenders are required to disclose certain information to borrowers regarding the terms and conditions of their loans.	In addition to existing requirements, eligible lenders subject to Title V-A of the Gramm-Leach-Bliley Act shall only use, release, disclose, sell, transfer, or give student information (e.g., name, address, social security number, or amount borrowed) as permitted by that subtitle. Eligible lenders, loan holders, and servicers must provide borrowers with certain information on borrower benefits they offer, such as interest rate reductions and any limitations on such benefits.
No similar provision.	Guaranty agencies working with IHEs they serve; and the Secretary working with IHEs in the DL program, must develop programs and materials for providing students with training on budgeting, financial management, debt management, and financial literacy. Such activities shall be considered default reduction activities for purposes of HEA, Section 422.
Eligible lenders may be disqualified for use of certain incentives.	Restrictions on inducement, payments, mailings, and advertising by eligible lenders are revised to address other items, such as payments for referrals, finder fees, prizes, stock or other securities, travel, entertainment expenses, tuition payment, and additional financial aid funds. The prohibition on unsolicited mailings is expanded to apply to mailings by postal or electronic means. Eligible lenders are prohibited from entering into consulting arrangements or other contracts with employees of IHEs' financial aid offices; and from performing any function the IHE is required to perform under HEA, Part B, D, or G. The compensation by lenders to students and employees of IHEs' financial aid offices is restricted.

Table 1. Continued

Current Law	S. 1642 (as reported by the **Senate Committee on Health, Education, Pensions, and Labor**)
IHEs may be eligible lenders; and eligible lenders may serve as trustees for IHEs.	This authority sunsets June 30, 2011.
FFEL and DL loans borrowers who die or become permanently and totally disabled (as determined in accordance with regulations) may have their loans discharged.	Specifies that borrowers who are unable to engage in gainful activity due to a medically determinable physical or mental impairment, expected to result in death, which has lasted or is expected to last continuously for 60 months, shall have their loans discharged.
Federal Work-Study (FWS) Programs.	
The allowance for books and supplies used in calculating each institution's average COA for the purpose of allocating funds according to the "fair share" allocation procedures is $450.	Increases the allowance for books and supplies to $600.
IHEs must use at least 7% of their FWS allocation to compensate students employed in community service; and must operate at least one tutoring or family literacy project. These requirements may be waived if the Secretary determines that enforcement would cause hardship for students at the IHE.	Revises the criteria upon which the Secretary may grant a waiver. Waivers would be granted because: enforcement would cause hardship for students at the IHE; or the IHE certifies that 15% or more of its full-time students participate in specified community service or tutoring and literacy activities.
IHEs may use not more than 10% or $50,000 of their FWS allocations for job location and development programs.	IHEs may use not more than 10% or $75,000 of their FWS allocations for job location and development programs.

Table 1. Continued

Current Law	S. 1642 (as reported by the Senate Committee on Health, Education, Pensions, and Labor)
Certain requirements apply to "work-learning" programs operated by work colleges.	Revises requirements applicable to work colleges, including (a) referring to programs as "comprehensive work-learning-service programs;" (b) limiting eligibility to public or profit four-year, degree-granting IHEs; and (c) requiring resident students to participate in comprehensive work-learning-service programs for not less than 5 hours per week, or 80 hours per period of enrollment.
Federal Perkins Loans.	
Perkins Loans may be cancelled for employment in certain types of public service jobs.	Expands occupations for which Perkins Loans may be cancelled to include (a) full-time staff member in a pre-kindergarten or child care program that is licensed or regulated by the state; (b) full-time faculty member at a TCU; (c) librarian with a master's degree in library science, and employed in a school served under Title I of the Elementary and Secondary Education Act, or a public library serving a Title I school; and (d) full-time speech language therapist with a master's degree working exclusively in Title I schools. Provides loan cancellation for these occupations, and for service as a member of the armed forces in an area of hostilities, at the rate of 15% for the 1st and 2nd years of service; 20% for the 3rd and 4th years of service; and 30% for the 5th year of service.

Table 1. Continued

Current Law	S. 1642 (as reported by the Senate Committee on Health, Education, Pensions, and Labor)
Perkins Loans borrowers of who die or become permanently and totally disabled (as determined in accordance with regulations) may have their loans discharged.	Specifies that borrowers who are unable to engage in gainful activity due to a medically determinable physical or mental impairment expected to result in death, which has lasted or is expected to last continuously for 60 months, shall have their loans discharged.
Need Analysis: Cost of Attendance.	
Defines an allowance for room and board costs incurred by a student without dependents who resides at home and for students who live on-campus in institutionally owned and operated housing.	Expands definition to include a room and board allowance for students who live in housing located on a military base or who receive a basic allowance for housing. The allowance would be based on the reasonable expenses incurred solely for board, not for room.
Need Analysis: Definitions.	
Untaxed Income and Benefits: The term untaxed income and benefits means, "... housing, food, and other allowances for military, clergy, and others."	Excludes the value of military housing or a military housing allowance received by a student or his/her parent, from consideration as untaxed income or benefits in the need analysis formula.
Definition of an Academic Year.	
On a case-by-case basis, the Secretary may reduce the minimum number of weeks of instruction in an academic year from 30 weeks to 26 weeks, for good cause, for IHEs providing a two-year or four-year program of instruction for which the institution awards an associate's or bachelor's degree.	Clarifies that the Secretary may only reduce the number of weeks of instruction for programs that measure program length in credit hours or clock hours. Thus, the Secretary may not waive the minimum weeks of instruction requirement for IHEs that solely measure student learning based on direct assessment.

Table 1. Continued

Current Law	S. 1642 (as reported by the Senate Committee on Health, Education, Pensions, and Labor)
Compliance Calendar.	
No similar provision.	Prior to the beginning of each award year, requires the Secretary to provide IHEs with a list of all reports and disclosures required under the HEA, including, for example, the date each report or disclosure is due, required recipients of each report or disclosure, and the required content of each report or disclosure.
Forms and Regulations.	
No similar provision.	Requires the Secretary to develop an EZ-Free Application for Federal Student Aid (FAFSA) for individuals eligible for automatic-zero expected family contribution (auto-zero EFC). The form shall only contain elements necessary to determine student eligibility for federal student aid and if applicant is eligible for auto-zero EFC. Secretary shall include state specific data on the EZ-FAFSA, if state allows residents to use EZ-FAFSA to apply for state aid.
No similar provision.	Develops a simplified electronic form for auto-zero EFC and simplified needs test (SMT)-eligible applicants. Secretary shall include state specific data on the simplified electronic version if State allows residents to use simplified version to apply for state aid.

Table 1. Continued

Current Law	S. 1642 (as reported by the Senate Committee on Health, Education, Pensions, and Labor)
No similar provision.	The Secretary shall phase-out printing the full paper FAFSA at such time as he/she determines it is not cost effective to print the full version. Prior to the phase-out and after, the Secretary shall maintain a paper form on the Internet. Any savings produced shall be used to help to improve access to electronic forms for students who qualify for auto-zero EFC.
No similar provision.	The Secretary shall encourage states to utilize the simplified forms to award state aid. States that do not permit the use of the forms must inform the Secretary of the reason(s) for not allowing. If State fails to inform the Secretary, Secretary can allow applicants from that state to complete the simplified application and not answer the state-specific questions.
No similar provision.	Within 180 days of the date of enactment, the Secretary shall implement a real-time data match between the Social Security Administration and ED to minimize the time required to receive a personal identification number.
No similar provision.	The Secretary shall determine, in cooperation with the states, IHEs and organizations involved in student financial assistance, the data elements that can be updated from the previous year's FAFSA.
No similar provision.	Applicants can complete FAFSA in the years prior to enrolling in postsecondary education to obtain a non-binding expected family contribution (EFC).

Table 1. Continued

Current Law	S. 1642 (as reported by the Senate Committee on Health, Education, Pensions, and Labor)
No similar provision.	The Secretary is authorized to include space for parent's social security number and date of birth on the FAFSA.
No similar provision.	Any entity that provides any value-added service such as completion or submission of the FAFSA shall provide a clear and conspicuous notice that the FAFSA is free; can be completed without professional assistance; and provide a link to ED's website. Also, cannot charge recipients who qualify for SNT or auto-zero EFC.
No similar provision.	The Secretary shall implement an early application demonstration study program that enables dependent students to complete a FAFSA two years prior to enrollment in an IHE. The Secretary shall partner with states, IHEs and secondary schools.
No similar provision.	The Secretary shall evaluate the demonstration program to measure the program's benefits and adverse effects. The evaluation should: identify whether financial awards or estimates, as applicable, have a positive impact on the higher education aspirations and plans of the student; determine whether using income data from two years prior would impact the state's and IHEs ability to make financial aid awards and commitments; focus on simplifying the financial aid application process; and developing alternative approaches to calculating the EFC.

Table 1. Continued

Current Law	S. 1642 (as reported by the Senate Committee on Health, Education, Pensions, and Labor)
No similar provision.	Upon conclusion of the study the Secretary in joint decision with the Secretary of the Treasury may use Internal Revenue Service data to pre-populate the FAFSA if such use would not negatively impact students, IHEs, states or the federal government on each of the following criteria: program costs; re-distributive effects on students; accuracy of aid determinations. Also should reduce burden to FAFSA filers.
Student Eligibility.	
A student who is not a high school graduate may be eligible for federal student aid and if it is determined that the student has the ability to benefit from postsecondary education based on the student's score on a specific examination, by meeting a state's standards for making this determination, or by completing secondary school through home schooling.	Allows IHEs to determine if a student has the ability to benefit from postsecondary education if the student satisfactorily completes six credit hours or the equivalent coursework applicable toward a degree or certificate offered by the IHE.
A student enrolled in a course of instruction at an IHE that is offered in whole or in part through telecommunications and leads to a recognized certificate or degree shall not be considered enrolled in correspondence courses.	Changes the current law reference to "distance education" to be consistent with the newly added definition of distance education and specifies that students enrolled in a course of instruction offered "principally through distance education" that leads to a recognized degree or certificate will not be considered enrolled in correspondence courses.

Table 1. Continued

Current Law	S. 1642 (as reported by the Senate Committee on Health, Education, Pensions, and Labor)
No similar provision.	Defines students with intellectual disabilities as a new group of students eligible for federal student aid. To be considered a student with intellectual disabilities, a student must be: (1) a person whose cognitive impairment substantially affects intellectual and cognitive functioning; (2) eligible for assistance under the Individuals with Disabilities Education Act (IDEA) and have completed secondary school or no longer be eligible for IDEA because he/she has exceeded the maximum age; (3) enrolled or accepted for enrollment in a comprehensive transition or postsecondary education program meeting specific requirements such as preparing students for gainful employment or independent living; and (4) satisfactorily progressing in the program based on institutional standards. The student must also meet various requirements related to federal aid repayment, citizenship or residency, and fraud with respect to Title IV programs.

Statute of Limitations and State Court Judgments.

Certain provisions ensure that obligations to repay loans and grant overpayments are enforced. For example, in collecting on a defaulted FFEL program loan, a guaranty agency or the Secretary shall not be subject to a defense raised by a borrower based on a claim of infancy.	Protects IHEs that participate in the Perkins Loan program against a defense raised by a borrower based on a claim of infancy. In the case of a deceased student, neither the student's estate nor the student's family's estate shall be required to repay any Title IV aid, student loan interest, or collection costs.

Table 1. Continued

Current Law	S. 1642 (as reported by the Senate Committee on Health, Education, Pensions, and Labor)
Institutional Refunds.	
If an IHE determines that a student did not begin the withdrawal process or failed to notify the institution of his/her intent to withdraw due to student illness, accident, or other circumstances beyond the student's control, the IHE may determine the appropriate withdrawal date.	Provides an IHE with the option of also determining that the HEA requirements related to the return of Title IV funds do not apply to the student.
Institutional and Financial Assistance Information for Students.	
No similar provision.	Requires IHEs to develop policies and sanctions related to copyright infringement.
No similar provision.	Requires IHEs to provide information on student body diversity, employment of graduates, and types of graduate and professional education pursued by graduates of four-year degree programs.
IHEs may exclude information on the graduation or completion rates of students who leave school to serve in the armed forces, on official church missions, or with a recognized foreign aid service of the federal government.	Adds that if these students represent 20% or more of certificate or degree-seeking, full-time, undergraduate students, the IHE may recalculate the completion and graduation rates of such students by excluding the time period during which they were not enrolled due to one of the reasons listed.
No similar provision.	Requires IHEs to disaggregate data on completion and graduation rates by gender, race/ethnicity, receipt of Pell, receipt of specific federal student loans, and receipt of other federal aid.

Table 1. Continued

Current Law	S. 1642 (as reported by the Senate Committee on Health, Education, Pensions, and Labor)
IHEs must provide exit counseling for borrowers.	Adds additional requirements to be discussed through exit counseling, including loan prepayment requirements, consequences of default, loan consolidation, and the National Student Loan Data System (NSLDS). Requires that the IHE provide the borrower with a "clear and conspicuous notice" regarding the effects of using a consolidation loan.
The Secretary must compile and disseminate information on state and other prepaid tuition and savings plans.	Requires the Secretary to also collect and disseminate information on state grant assistance.
IHEs may exclude from their reports on the completion and graduation rates of students and student athletes, students or student athletes who leave school to serve in the armed forces, on official church missions, or with a recognized foreign aid service of the federal government.	Adds that if these students represent 20% or more of certificate or degree-seeking, full-time, undergraduate students, the IHE may recalculate the completion and graduation rates of such students by excluding the time period during which they were not enrolled due to one of the reasons listed.
All IHEs participating in Title IV must disclose their campus security policies and campus crime statistics.	Excludes foreign institutions from this requirement.
No similar provision.	Requires IHEs to include a statement of their policies regarding immediate emergency response and evacuation procedures. Among other things, these policies must include procedures to test emergency response and evacuation procedures annually.

Table 1. Continued

Current Law	S. 1642 (as reported by the Senate Committee on Health, Education, Pensions, and Labor)
No similar provision.	Requires the Secretary to annually report to the authorizing committees regarding institutional compliance with the disclosure of campus security policies and crime statistics, and the Secretary's monitoring of such compliance.
No similar provision.	Requires IHEs to publicly disclose their transfer of credit policies, and to state whether transfer of credit is denied solely on the basis of the accreditation held by the sending institution. IHEs must also publish a list of IHEs with which it has established articulation agreements.
No similar provision.	Prohibits the Secretary or the Accreditation and Institutional Quality and Integrity Advisory Committee (formerly NACIQI) from requiring particular policies, procedures, or practices by IHEs regarding transfer of credit.
No similar provision.	States that the transfer of credit policy does not: (1) permit ED to exercise any direction, supervision, or control over the curriculum, instruction, administration, or personnel at any IHE or over any accrediting agency; (2) limit the application of the General Education Provisions Act ; or (3) provide students with legally enforceable rights to require an IHE to accept a transfer of credit.
No similar provision.	Requires IHEs to annually disclose information on fire safety practices and standards.

Table 1. Conntinued

Current Law	S. 1642 (as reported by the Senate Committee on Health, Education, Pensions, and Labor)
National Student Loan Data System (NSLDS).	
The Secretary is required to establish in NSLDS, information regarding loans made under the FFEL, DL, and federal Perkins Loan programs.	Requires the Secretary to take certain actions with regard to NSLDS. These include ensuring: NSLDS is used for legitimate purposes; that non-governmental researchers and policy analysts are prohibited from accessing personally identifiable information; that students are informed of their rights and responsibilities about information contained in NSLDS on aid received under Title IV; that loan recipients are informed that information about their loans may be accessible to authorized NSLDS users; and that standardized protocols are developed for limiting access to NSLDS.
Early Awareness of Financial Aid Eligibility.	
No similar provision.	The Secretary, in cooperation with states, IHEs, secondary and middle schools, and outreach programs, shall implement an early awareness of financial aid information program. ED should also develop a paper and electronic means of allowing applicants to receive a non-binding estimate of the amount of grant and loan aid he/she may be eligible for.
Program Participation Agreement (PPA).	
No similar provision.	Requires IHEs to establish and make publicly available a code of conduct regarding student loans that addresses issues such as, revenue sharing, contracting arrangements, and advisory board compensation.

Table 1. Continued

Current Law	S. 1642 (as reported by the Senate Committee on Health, Education, Pensions, and Labor)
Proprietary institutions are required to earn 10% of their revenue from non-Title IV sources of revenue as a condition of institutional eligibility; also referred to as the 90/10 rule.	Moves the 90/10 rule from Title I to the PPA, and subjects proprietary institutions violating this rule to sanctions. By making this change, the 90/10 rule is no longer an institutional eligibility requirement.
No similar provision.	Adds requirements related to preferred lender lists maintained by IHEs. For example, IHEs must disclose why each lender is on the preferred lender list.
No similar provision.	Adds requirements for IHEs related to teach-outs. Defines a teach-out plan as a written plan providing for the equitable treatment of students if an IHE ceases operations before all students have completed their program of study.
No similar provision.	Requires that IHEs that violate their code of conduct regarding students loans have their eligibility to participate in the federal student loan programs limited, suspended, or terminated.
Regulatory Relief and Improvement: Quality Assurance Program.	
The Secretary's authority for the QAP expired June 30, 1999.	The Secretary has authority to continue existing programs and establish additional experimental sites until June 30, 2008. Also requires the Secretary to review and submit a biennial report to the authorizing committees on the experience of participating IHEs.
Transfer of Allotments.	
IHEs may transfer up to 25% of their Perkins Loan FCC allotment to FSEOG and/or FWS; and up to 25% of their FWS allotment to FSEOG.	Allows IHEs to transfer up to 25% of their FSEOG allotment to FWS.

Table 1. Continued

Current Law	S. 1642 (as reported by the Senate Committee on Health, Education, Pensions, and Labor)
Advisory Committee on Student Financial Assistance (ACSFA).	
ACSFA currently provides extensive knowledge and understanding of federal, state, and institutional programs for postsecondary student assistance, among other things.	Expands the purpose of the ACSFA to include providing knowledge and understanding of early intervention programs and making recommendations that will result in early awareness for low and moderate-income students of their eligibility for assistance.
No similar provision.	Requires the ACSFA to conduct a study of innovative pathways to baccalaureate degree attainment, such as dual enrollment, Pell program changes, and compressed or modular scheduling, among other things.
Recognition of Accrediting Agency or Association.	
Accrediting agencies are required to consistently apply and enforce standards to ensure courses and programs are of sufficient quality to achieve their stated objectives for the duration of the accreditation period.	Requires accrediting agencies to consider the stated mission of the institution, including religious missions, when applying and enforcing standards.
No similar provision.	Requires an accrediting agency that already has or seeks to include the evaluation of distance education programs within its scope of recognition to demonstrate to the Secretary that its standards effectively address the quality of distance education programs in the same areas in which it evaluates classroom-based programs. It does not require IHEs to have separate standards for courses or programs offered by distance education.

Table 1. Continued

Current Law	S. 1642 (as reported by the Senate Committee on Health, Education, Pensions, and Labor)
No similar provision.	Requires an accrediting agency to require that IHEs offering distance education programs establish that a student registered for a distance education course is the same student that participates in, completes, and receives credit for the course.
Accrediting agencies are required to assess the IHE's success regarding student achievement in relation to the institution's mission, including, as appropriate, course completion, state licensing exams, and job placement rates.	Requires accrediting agencies to examine an IHE's success regarding student achievement in relation to the institution's mission, which may include different standards for different institutions or programs. In making this assessment, accrediting agencies must examine achievement based on expected levels of student achievement established by the institution and which use empirical evidence and external indicators, as appropriate, to examine:
	• student retention rates;
	• course completion rates;
	• program completion and graduation rates; for prebaccalaureate career and technical education programs, degree programs leading to initial professional licensure or certification, the results of state licensing exams and job
	• placement rates;
	• enrollment in graduate or professional programs; and
	• other student performance information selected by the institution, especially information used by the institution to evaluate or strengthen its programs and information that reflects the institution's mission and distinctive goals for students.

Table 1. Continued

Current Law	S. 1642 (as reported by the Senate Committee on Health, Education, Pensions, and Labor)
An institution may oppose actions taken by its accrediting agency that adversely affect the institution. Specifically, accrediting agencies are required to apply procedures throughout the accrediting process that comply with due process including:	Modifies due process requirements for an institution opposing an adverse action to include:
• adequate specification of requirements and deficiencies at the IHE or program being evaluated; • notice of an opportunity for a hearing by any such IHE; • right to appeal an adverse action against any such IHE; and • right to representation by counsel for any such IHE.	• adequate specification of requirements and deficiencies at the IHE or program being evaluated; • opportunity for a written response by any such IHE that would be included, prior to final action, in the evaluation and withdrawal proceedings; • upon written request by the IHE, an opportunity for the IHE to appeal any adverse action at a hearing prior to the action becoming final, before an appeals panel that does not include members of the accrediting agency's decision-making body that made the adverse decision and that is subject to a conflict of interest policy; and • right to representation by counsel for any such IHE during an appeal of an adverse action.

Table 1. Continued

Current Law	S. 1642 (as reported by the Senate Committee on Health, Education, Pensions, and Labor)
An accrediting agency must make a summary of any review that results in final denial, termination, or suspension of accreditation, and the comments of the affected institution, available to the public, upon request, and to the Secretary and state licensing or authorizing agency. No similar provision.	Requires the agency to make the summary publicly available and available to the state licensing or authorizing agency, and submit to the Secretary, a summary of agency actions including: • the award of accreditation or reaccreditation; • final denial, withdrawal, suspension, or termination of accreditation, or placement on probation of an IHE, and any findings made in relation to the action taken, and any official comments of the affected IHE; and • any other adverse action taken with respect to an IHE. Requires on-site evaluations to include a review of the federally required information that the institution or program must provide to current and prospective students.
No similar provision.	Requires accrediting agencies to monitor the growth of programs at IHEs that are experiencing significant enrollment growth.
No similar provision.	Requires an IHE to submit a teach-out plan for approval by the accrediting agency if specific events occur, such as the accrediting agency withdraws accreditation or the IHE notifies the accrediting agency that it will be closing.
No similar provision.	Requires accrediting agencies, as part of accreditation or re-accreditation reviews, to confirm that the IHE has publicly disclosed its transfer of credit policy and that the policy specifically states whether the transfer of credit is denied solely on the basis of the accreditation of the sending institution.

Table 1. Continued

Current Law	S. 1642 (as reported by the Senate Committee on Health, Education, Pensions, and Labor)
No similar provision.	Prohibits the Secretary from establishing any criteria that "specifies, denies, or prescribes" the standards an accrediting agency will use to assess an institution's success with respect to student achievement.
Program Review and Data.	
The Secretary must conduct program reviews.	Adds that the Secretary must provide an IHE with an adequate opportunity to review and respond to any program review report and relevant materials before a final program review is issued. This review and response must be taken into consideration in any final program review or audit determination an IHE's response. The report or determination must include a written statement addressing the IHE's response, a statement of the basis for the determination, and a copy of the IHE's response. The confidentiality of any program review report must be maintained until these steps are taken and a final program review is issued, except to inform the state or accrediting agency when the Secretary takes an action against an IHE. Requires the Secretary to promptly disclose all program review reports to the institution under consideration.

Table 1. Continued

Current Law	S. 1642 (as reported by the Senate Committee on Health, Education, Pensions, and Labor)
Timely Information About Loans.	
No similar provision.	Requires lenders of a loan made, insured, or guaranteed under Title IV to provide specific information to the borrower at designated times, including pertinent information about the loan for each payment installment period, information at least one month prior to the commencement of repayment, information provided during delinquency, and information provided at least twice during default.
Title V: Developing Institutions.	
Hispanic Serving Institutions (HSIs).	
No similar provision.	Expands authorized activities to include education or counseling services designed to improve financial literacy and economic literacy of students or students' parents and articulation agreements and student support programs designed to facilitate the transfer from a two-year IHE to a four-year IHE.
No similar provision.	Establishes the Promoting Postbaccalaureate Opportunities for Hispanic Students. The program would provide competitive grants for HSIs offering postbaccalaureate degrees and certificates. Program would be similar in nature to the existing program for HBCUs.

Table 1. Continued

Current Law	S. 1642 (as reported by the Senate Committee on Health, Education, Pensions, and Labor)
Title VI: International Education Programs.	
International and Foreign Language Studies.	
Supports centers, programs, and fellowships in U.S. IHEs, including programs partnering with overseas institutions, to increase the number of trained personnel, and study in foreign language and area studies.	Requires the Secretary to consult with appropriate federal agencies to determine national priorities and assist programs funded under this title to develop surveys of participants to determine placement after graduation.
Grants may be used for a variety of activities to improve instruction including teaching and research materials, curriculum planning and development, linkages with foreign institutions, summer institutes, travel support, visiting scholars, and professional development.	Adds to the list of authorized activities "support for instructors of less commonly taught languages" as well as "programs of linkage or outreach between or among" State and local educational agencies and federal or state scholarship programs.
Fellowship recipients must be graduate students engaged in, "the international aspects of a professional studies program, including, pre-dissertation level studies, preparation for dissertation research, dissertation research abroad, and dissertation writing."	Removes the graduate student limitation and makes undergraduate students engaged in intermediate or advanced study eligible for a fellowship.
Only 10% of total Title VI, Part A appropriation may be used to support undergraduate programs.	Increases the amount to 20% of total Title VI, Part A appropriations, but the study abroad component is limited to 10%.
Authorizes the Secretary to conduct research that contributes to achieving the purposes of Title VI, Part A.	Adds to the description of this research, "evaluations of the extent to which programs funded under this title reflect diverse perspectives and generate debate on world regions and international affairs."

Table 1. Continued

Current Law	S. 1642 (as reported by the Senate Committee on Health, Education, Pensions, and Labor)
Authorizes the Secretary to establish the Institute for International Public Policy to increase the number of African Americans and underrepresented minorities in international service.	Authorizes the provision of financial assistance to needy students in the form of summer stipends of up to $3,000 or Ralph Bunche scholarships of up to $5,000 per academic year.

Title VII: Graduate and Postsecondary Improvement Programs.

Graduate Student and Program Assistance.

Jacob K. Javits Fellowship Program — The Secretary is authorized to award fellowships for graduate study in the arts, humanities, and social sciences.	Requires that the Fellowship Board include members from diverse institutions and geographic regions and at least one member from an institution eligible for a grant under Titles III or V.
Graduate Assistance in Areas of National Need (GAANN) — The Secretary is authorized to award grants to IHEs and other entities to support graduate programs in areas of national need.	Amends procedure for designating areas of national need, specifying consultation with the National Science Foundation, the Departments of Defense and Homeland Security, the National Academy of Sciences, and the BLS.
Thurgood Marshall Legal Educational Opportunity Program — The Secretary is authorized to award grants to provide low-income, minority, or disadvantaged college students with financial assistance to gain access to and complete law school.	Expands scope of authorized activities to include service to secondary school students, to emphasize undergraduates' preparation for admission to law school, and to pay stipends to participants.

Fund for the Improvement of Postsecondary Education (FIPSE).

The Secretary is authorized to make grants and enter into awards for contracts under FIPSE.	Adds authorized uses of funds to include (1) establish and continue technologically-mediated collaborations; (2) reform remedial and English language instruction; and (3) create consortia of IHEs to establish interdisciplinary programs on poverty.

Table 1. Continued

Current Law	S. 1642 (as reported by the Senate Committee on Health, Education, Pensions, and Labor)
No similar provision.	Establishes a new FIPSE program to support integrated secondary-postsecondary graduation reform programs, with funds going to Project GRAD USA (a non-profit).
No similar provision.	Establishes a new FIPSE program to create, at an IHE, a Center for Best Practices to Support Single-Parent Students.
No similar provision.	Establishes a new FIPSE program to create, at an IHE, a clearinghouse for Understanding the Federal Regulatory Impact on Higher Education.
Urban Community Service Program.	
Program provides funds to IHEs in urban areas to enable them to work with organizations to devise and implement solutions to the problems in their communities.	Repeals this program.
Demonstration Projects to Ensure Students with Disabilities Receive a Quality Higher Education.	
Program provides funds to support demonstration projects that provide technical assistance and professional development for faculty and administrators in IHEs to provide individuals with disabilities a quality postsecondary education.	Expands the list of authorized activities to include the development of innovative teaching methods and strategies to ensure the smooth transition of students with disabilities from high school to postsecondary education; and strategies to make distance education programs or classes more available to students with disabilities.
No similar provision.	Adds a new subpart that establishes a grant program and coordinating center transition programs for students with intellectual disabilities.

Table 1. Continued

Current Law	S. 1642 (as reported by the Senate Committee on Health, Education, Pensions, and Labor)
S. 1642, Title VIII: Miscellaneous.	
Mathematics and Science Scholars Program.	
No similar provision.	Establishes a new grant program that authorizes the Secretary to award competitive grants to states. States would award $1,000 to first and second-year undergraduate students who complete a rigorous high school program in math and science. States must match 50% of federal funds and may set priorities (e.g., underrepresented groups) for the scholarships.
Postsecondary Education Assessment.	
No similar provision.	The Secretary must contract with a bipartisan organization to study the cost factors associated with tuition at IHEs. Provision does not specify authorization for funding
Job Skill Training in High-Growth Occupations or Industries.	
No similar provision.	Establishes a new program that authorizes the Secretary to award competitive grants to IHEs and local workforce board partnerships for development of job training programs in high-growth industries.
Additional Capacity for R.N. Students or Graduate-Level Nursing Students.	
No similar provision.	Establishes a new program that authorizes the Secretary to award competitive grants to nursing programs to expand faculty and facilities. Necessary funding is indefinitely authorized.

Table 1. Continued

Current Law	S. 1642 (as reported by the Senate Committee on Health, Education, Pensions, and Labor)
American History for Freedom.	
No similar provision.	Creates a new program that authorizes the Secretary to award competitive grants to IHEs to establish or strengthen programs that promote "(1) traditional American history; (2) the history and nature of, and threats to, free institutions; or (3) the history and achievements of Western Civilization."
Teach For America.	
No similar provision.	The Secretary is authorized to award a grant to Teach For America, Inc., to implement and expand its program of recruiting, selecting, training, and supporting new teacher; and to study the program's effectiveness. The organization may not use federal funds for more than 25% of its administrative costs.
Patsy T. Mink Fellowship Program.	
No similar provision.	Establishes a new program to award competitive grants to IHEs for fellowships to minorities and women seeking doctoral degrees with the intent of entering the professoriate. Fellowship recipients must sign a service agreement. At least 30% of funds would be reserved for IHEs eligible for a grant under Titles III or V.

Table 1. Continued

Current Law	S. 1642 (as reported by the Senate Committee on Health, Education, Pensions, and Labor)
Improving College Enrollment by Secondary Schools.	
No similar provision.	The Secretary must contract with a non-profit organization to conduct a needs assessment and provide comprehensive services to urban school districts and rural states in order to improve college-going rates of participating schools.
Predominantly Black Institutions (PBIs).	
No similar provision.	The Secretary is authorized to award formula grants of not less than $250,000 to eligible predominantly black IHEs to develop programs to enhance capacity to serve low- and middle-income Black American students. A PBI is an IHE that enrolls at least 1,000 undergraduates, of which at least 40% must be African-American and not less than 50% must be low-income or first-generation and 50% must be pursuing an associate's or bachelor's degree. Allowable grant activities are similar to those authorized under Title III, Part B. Grantees may not concurrently receive Title III Part A or B funds.

Table 1. Continued

Current Law	S. 1642 (as reported by the Senate Committee on Health, Education, Pensions, and Labor)
Early Childhood Education Professional Development and Career Task Force.	
No similar provision.	Authorizes the Secretary to award competitive grants to states to establish task forces to develop comprehensive statewide plans for professional development and careers for early childhood education providers, and which shall include assistance to pay up to $17,500 for professional development for individuals with incomes below the median income and who sign service agreements to work in early childhood education programs.
Improving Science, Technology, Engineering, and Mathematics (STEM) Education with a Focus on Alaska Native and Native Hawaiian Students.	
No similar provision.	Authorizes the Secretary to award competitive grants to partnerships (STEM schools/colleges, two-year IHEs, and private career organizations) to develop or expand STEM programs and academic support services and internships for STEM students, with a focus on Alaska Native and Native Hawaiian students.
Pilot Program to Increase Persistence in Community Colleges.	
No similar provision.	The Secretary is authorized to award competitive grants to IHEs for scholarships ($2,000 per year for two years) and counseling services for low-income students with dependents. Scholarship funds are paid upon completion of specified academic milestones. The program is to be evaluated with random assignment.

Table 1. Continued

Current Law	S. 1642 (as reported by the Senate Committee on Health, Education, Pensions, and Labor)
Student Safety and Campus Emergency Management.	
No similar provision.	The Secretary, in consultation with the Attorney General and the Secretary of Homeland Security, is authorized to award competitive grants to IHEs, to be matched by non-federal sources, for emergency communication systems or improved safety training and response. The Secretaries and Attorney General may also advise IHEs on model emergency response practices.
S. 1642, Title IX: Amendments to Other Laws.	
Education of the Deaf Act of 1986 (EDA).	
Section 104 of the EDA refers to elementary and secondary education programs.	Renames the section the "Laurent Clerc National Deaf Education Center" and all references to elementary and secondary education programs are replaced by references to the "Clerc Center."
No similar provision.	Creates an additional requirement to the subsection on "Administrative requirements" requiring Gallaudet University to select and implement academic standards and assessments for programs at the Center and determine and publicize whether programs are making adequate yearly progress based on these standards.
Authorizes the National Technical Institute for the Deaf (NTID).	The current operator of the center, Rochester Institute of Technology (RIT) would be specified in the act

Table 1. Continued

Current Law	S. 1642 (as reported by the Senate Committee on Health, Education, Pensions, and Labor)
No similar provision.	Requires the Secretary to re-compete the operation of NTID if RIT terminates the agreement.
No similar provision.	Creates a new section that authorizes the Secretary to make grants to eligible non-profit entities for "cultural experiences" for deaf and hard-of-hearing children and adults
Provides for enrollment of international students at Gallaudet and NTID and caps the number of such students.	Adds a new provision exempting international students participating in distance learning through Gallaudet or NTID from counting against the enrollment cap except that such students shall not displace a U.S. citizen applying for such courses. In addition, international students participating in distance learning would not be charged the tuition surcharge other international students at these institutions must pay.
International students must pay a tuition surcharge of 100% except for certain students from "developing countries" for whom the institution may reduce the surcharge to 50%.	The 100% surcharge would be continued for students from "non-developing countries." The 50% surcharge for students from "developing countries" would be mandated, rather than being at the institution's discretion for certain students. Beginning with the 2008-2009 academic year, the surcharges would be reduced to 50% and 25%, respectively, for students who demonstrate "need" and make "a good faith effort" to obtain aid from their home governments.
"Developing country" is defined as having not more than a per capita income of $4,000 in 1990 dollars.	Definition would be updated to $4,825 in 1999 dollars.

Table 1. Continued

Current Law	S. 1642 (as reported by the Senate Committee on Health, Education, Pensions, and Labor)
Higher Education Amendments of 1998.	
The Secretary is required to conduct numerous studies of selected topics.	Repeals provisions for the following studies: • Study of Market Mechanisms in the Federal Student Loan programs • Study of the Feasability of Alternative Financial Instruments for Determining Lender Yields • Student Related Debt Study • Study of Transfer of Credits • Study of Opportunities for Participation in Athletics Programs • Study of the Effectiveness of Cohort Default Rates for Institutions with few Student Loan Borrowers • Education Welfare Study
Title VIII authorizes various types of programs, and includes a Sense of the Congress regarding good character.	Repeals the following programs and provisions: ! Community Scholarship Mobilization; ! Improving United States Understanding of Science Engineering and Technology in East Asia ! Sense of the Congress regarding good character
Grants to States for Workplace and Community Transition Training for Incarcerated Youth Offenders.	
Youth are currently defined as persons 25 or younger.	Changes the definition of "youth" to include persons under the age of 35.

Table 1. Continued

Current Law	S. 1642 (as reported by the Senate Committee on Health, Education, Pensions, and Labor)
Each state can receive $1,500 maximum, annually for each eligible student for tuition, books, and essential materials.	Increases the amount that each state can receive for each eligible student to $3,000 annually, for tuition, books, and essential materials.
Tribally Controlled College or University Assistance Act of 1978.	
No similar provision.	Defines "Indian student" to mean a student who is: a member of an Indian tribe; or a biological child of a member of an Indian tribe.
No similar provision.	Expands the definition of an eligible grantee to specify that the tribally controlled college must also be accredited by a nationally recognized accrediting association or an association recognized by the Secretary.
Grant amount of $6,000 per Indian student.	Increases the grant amount per Indian student count to $8,000.
No similar provision.	Creates a new Subtitle V on Tribally Controlled Postsecondary Career and Technical Institutions. "Tribally controlled postsecondary career and technical institution" aligns with the definition of the term in the Carl D. Perkins Career and Technical Education Act.
Navajo Community College Act.	
The purpose of the act is to provide support for the education of members of the Navajo tribe, by supporting the Navajo Community College.	Strikes Navajo Community College and specifies that the support will be directed to Diné College.

Appendix A. Outline of the Higher Education Act: Titles, Parts, Programs, and Major Provisions

Title I: General Provisions

Part A: Definitions
Institutions of Higher Education (IHEs)
Institutions of Higher Education for Title IV Purposes

Part B: Additional General Provisions
Antidiscrimination
Protection of Student Speech and Association Rights
National Advisory Committee on Institutional Quality and Integrity (NACIQI)
Disclosure of Foreign Gifts
Collegiate Initiative to Reduce Binge Drinking and Illegal Alcohol Consumption

Part C: Cost of Higher Education
Market Information and Public Accountability

Part D: Administrative Provisions for Delivery of Student Financial Assistance
Performance-Based Organization [Federal Student Aid]

Title II: Teacher Quality Enhancement

Part A: Teacher Quality Enhancement Grants for States and Partnerships
Teacher Quality Enhancement State Grants
Teacher Quality Enhancement Partnership Grants
Teacher Recruitment Grants

Part B: Preparing Tomorrow's Teachers to Use Technology
Technology Training Grants

Title III: Institutional Aid

Part A: Strengthening Institutions
Strengthening Institutions Grants
Tribal Colleges and Universities (TCUs) Grants
Alaska Native and Native Hawaiian-serving Institutions Grants

Part B: Strengthening Historically Black Colleges and Universities (HBCUs)
Strengthening Historically Black Colleges and Universities Grants
Strengthening Historically Black Graduate Institutions Grants

Part C: Endowment Challenge Grants for Part A and Part B Institutions
Endowment Challenge Grants

Part D: Historically Black College and University Capital Financing
Federal Insurance for Bonds
Historically Black College and University Capital Financing Board

Part E: Minority Science and Engineering Improvement Program
Minority Institutions Science Improvement Program

Part F: General Provisions

TITLE IV: STUDENT ASSISTANCE

Part A: Grants to Students in Attendance at Institutions of Higher Education

Federal Pell Grants
Academic Competitiveness Grants
National Science and Mathematics Access to Retain Talent (SMART) Grants
Federal TRIO Programs
    Talent Search
    Upward Bound
    Student Support Services
    Ronald E. McNair Postbaccalaureate Achievement Program
    Educational Opportunity Centers
Gaining Early Awareness and Readiness for Undergraduate Programs (GEAR UP)
Academic Achievement Scholarships
Federal Supplemental Educational Opportunity Grants (FSEOG)
Leveraging Educational Assistance Partnership (LEAP) Program
Special Leveraging Educational Assistance Partnership (SLEAP) Program
College Assistance Migrant Program
Robert C. Byrd Honors Scholarship Program
Child Care Access Means Parents in School
Learning Anytime Anywhere Partnerships

Part B: Federal Family Education Loans (FFEL)

Robert T. Stafford Federal Loan Program
    Federal Stafford Loans
    Federal PLUS Loans
    Federal Consolidation Loans
    Federal Unsubsidized Stafford Loans
FFEL/Guaranteed Student Loan Program Provisions
    Insurance Fund
    Interest Rates, Terms, Conditions, and Benefits
    Interest Subsidies
    Guaranty Agency Agreements
Targeted Loan Terms
    Armed Forces Student Loan Interest Payment Program
    Loan Forgiveness for Teachers

Loan and Grant Repayment
Institutional Refunds
Institutional and Financial Assistance Information for Students
Collegiate Athletics Information Disclosures.
Jeanne Cleary Disclosure of Security Policy and Campus Crime
    Statistics Act
National Student Loan Data System (NSLDS)
College Access Initiative
Distance Education Demonstration Programs
Program Participation Agreements (PPA)
Integrated Postsecondary Student Aid Survey (IPEDS)
Quality Assurance Program
Regulatory Improvement and Streamlining Experiments
Wage Garnishment
Advisory Committee on Student Financial Assistance
Negotiated Rulemaking

Part H: Program Integrity
Program Integrity Triad
    State Role
    Accrediting Agency Recognition
    Eligibility and Certification Procedures.

Title V: Developing Institutions

Part A: Hispanic Serving Institutions (HSIs)
Developing Hispanic Serving Institutions Grants

Part B: General Provisions

Title VI: International Education Programs

Part A: International and Foreign Language Studies
National and Area Language Centers and Programs
Graduate Fellowships for Foreign Language and Area or International
    Studies
Language Resource Centers
Undergraduate International Studies and Foreign Language Programs

Technological Information and Cooperation for Foreign Information Access
American Overseas Research Centers

Part B: Business and International Education Programs
Centers for International Business Education
Business and International Education and Training Programs

Part C: Institute for International Public Policy
Institute for International Public Policy

Part D: General Provisions

Title VII: Graduate and Postsecondary Education Improvement Programs

Part A: Graduate Education Programs
Jacob K. Javits Fellowship Program
Graduate Assistance in Areas of National Need (GAANN)
Thurgood Marshall Legal Educational Opportunity Program

Part B: Fund for the Improvement of Postsecondary Education (FIPSE)
Fund for the Improvement of Postsecondary Education Grants

Part C: Urban Community Service
Urban Community Service Grants

Part D: Demonstration Projects to Ensure Students with Disabilities Receive a Quality Higher Education
Quality Higher Education for Students with Disabilities Grants

Additional Programs Authorized by Higher Education Amendments

Higher Education Amendments of 1986.
   Title XV — American Indian, Alaska Native, and Native Hawaiian Culture and Art Development
   Institute of American Indian and Alaska Native Culture and Arts Development
   Program for Native Hawaiian and Alaska Native Culture and Arts Development

Higher Education Amendments of 1992.
   Title XV — Related Programs and Amendments to Other Laws
   B.J. Stupak Olympic Scholarships

Higher Education Amendments of 1998.
   Title VIII — Studies, Reports, and Related Programs
   Community Scholarship Mobilization Grants
   Grants to States for Workplace and Community Transition Training for Incarcerated Youth Offenders
   Grants to Combat Violent Crimes Against Women on Campuses
   Improving United States Understanding of Science, Engineering, and Technology in East Asia
   Underground Railroad Educational and Cultural Program

Notes: As amended through September 30, 2006. Programs are in *italic* type. Authorizations for demonstration, dissemination, professional development, research, study, or evaluation grants and contracts are not delineated above. Expired programs or provisions are omitted.

REFERENCES

[1]   The College Board, Trends in Student Aid 2006.

[2]   The original termination date for most of the provisions of the HEA was September 30, 2003, which was the original date enacted by the Higher Education Amendments of 1998. This termination date was extended through FY2004 by the General Education Provisions Act (GEPA). A series of subsequent measures — P.L. 108-366, P.L. 109-81, P.L. 109-150, P.L. 109-212. P.L. 109-238, and P.L. 109-292 — have temporarily extended the HEA program and provision authority.

[3]   For additional information about the budget reconciliation process see CRS Report RL34077, *Student Loans, Student Aid, and FY2008 Budget Reconciliation*, by Adam Stoll, David P. Smole, and Charmaine Mercer.

[4]   This report will be updated to include a column for the House version of the HEA reauthorization should a measure gain passage during the 110th Congress.

INDEX

D

E

F

W